Minibeasts

Written by Siobhan Hardy

Photography by Steve Lumb

Collins

A snail.

A spider.

A worm.

A caterpillar.

A butterfly.

A ladybird.

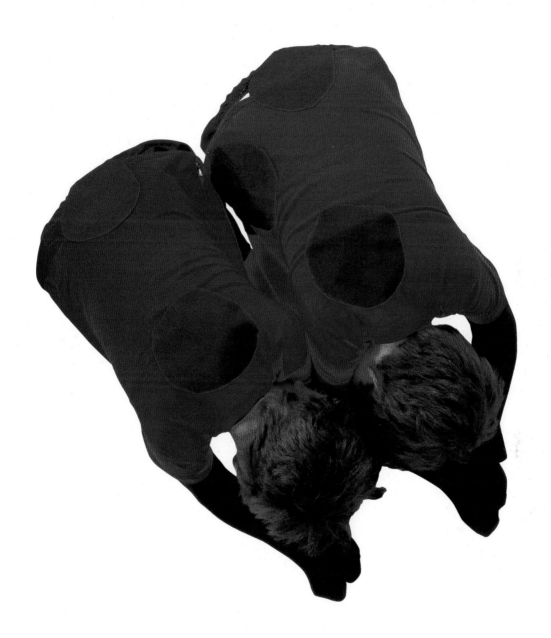

Minibeasts

a snail

a spider

a worm

a caterpillar

a butterfly

a ladybird

15

 Ideas for reading

Written by Linda Pagett B.Ed (hons), M.Ed
Lecturer and Educational Consultant

Reading objectives:
- read some common irregular words
- read and understand simple sentences
- use phonic knowledge to decode regular words and read them aloud accurately
- demonstrate understanding when talking with others about what they have read

Communication and language objectives:
- listen attentively in a range of situations
- express themselves effectively, showing awareness of listeners' needs
- give their attention to what others say and respond appropriately

- develop their own narratives and explanations by connecting ideas or events

Curriculum links: Knowledge and understanding of the world; Creative development

High frequency words: a

Interest words: minibeasts, snail, spider, worm, caterpillar, butterfly, ladybird

Word count: 12

Resources: activities are suggested that will require art and P.E. facilities

Build a context for reading

- Look at the cover of the book together. Use the terms 'cover' and 'title'. Read the title 'Minibeasts' to them and then discuss what minibeasts are. Ask them to name some minibeasts.

- Read the title together, and observe children matching spoken word to printed word.

- Walk through the book, and ask children to discuss what is in the pictures. Talk about the pattern of minibeast photos and children's minibeast shapes. On p3, what are the children trying to do? (form the shape of a snail). Discuss how the children make minibeast shapes by arranging their bodies carefully. Their clothes make them look like the minibeast, too.

Understand and apply reading strategies

- Ask children to read the book aloud and independently up to p13.

- Observe, prompt and praise the children's use of one-to-one matching, left-right scanning, fluent reading of 'a' and using picture cues to read the minibeast names. If children have difficulty with the minibeast words, prompt them to look closely at the pictures and the initial letter.

- Ask children to look at the children's shapes on the right hand pages and to point out the different parts of the minibeast, e.g. head, legs, spots.